NUMBER 521

THE ENGLISH EXPERIENCE

ITS RECORD IN EARLY PRINTED BOOKS
PUBLISHED IN FACSIMILE

The publishers acknowledge their gratitude to
the Curators of the Bodleian Library, Oxford
for their permission to reproduce the
Library's copy, Shelfmark: Wood.C.35.

S.T.C.No. 11683

Collation: A-H^4

Published in 1973 by

Theatrum Orbis Terrarum Ltd.,
O.Z. Voorburgwal 85, Amsterdam

&

Da Capo Press Inc.
- a subsidiary of Plenum Publishing Corporation -
277 West 17th Street, New York N.Y. 1011

Printed in the Netherlands

ISBN 90 221 0521 0

Library of Congress Catalog Card Number:
72-5996

THE
Defence of Militarie
profeſsion.

Wherein is eloquently ſhewed
the due commendation of Martiall
proweſſe, and plainly prooued
how neceſſary the exerciſe
of Armes is for this
our age.

IMPRIN-
ted at London by Hen-
ry Middleton, for
Iohn Hariſon.

1579.

¶ TO THE RIGHT
honorable, *Edward de Vere*, Earle of
Oxenford, vicount Bulbecke, Lord of Escales
and Baldesmere, and Lord great Cham-
berlaine of England.

Xperience bea-
reth such a soueraigntie
ouer all thinges humane
and diuine, that without
it the quality or power either of worde, deede, de-
uise, or matter, cannot
make it selfe knowen to
the vnderstanding of mē:
for the heauenly trueth iustifieth it selfe by the effects
of his nature and power, made apparant to the eyes &
capacities of earthly creatures.

Adam not well staid vpō the trueth of Gods word,
transgressed the cōmandement, & feeling the plagues
of his offence, had thereby experience of the power &
trueth of his Almightie Creator.

The first worlde ouerflowing in wickednesse, was
drowned in the flood of Gods vengeance: to geeue
experience to the world that ensued, what it is to contemne his worde and Prophets.

A 2 *Noah*

Noah beleeued the word of the Lord, and obeying his commandement, prepared the Arke & was saued in the flood, he & all his family: by experience wherof the world is made to vnderstand the power and assurance of Gods trueth and fauour towarde his elect people.

The Lord willed *Moses* to denounce his plagues againſt Egypt, and in the effect of his power & trueth he accompliſhed the ſame vpon man and beaſt, vpon fruit and tree, vpon earth and water: the experience whereof made *Moses* and the Iſraelites ſo hardie in fayth, that they tooke their way through the red Sea, as through the fieldes on drie land.

Pharao in the hardneſſe of his heart purſued the Iſraelites, and was drowned, he and all his armie in the pathes where *Iacob* went drye ſhod: whereby all the kings and princes of the earth had & haue experience, what it is to contemne God, to perſecute his people, & to deſpiſe his worde and miniſters.

The like experience made *Iosuah* bolde to lead Iſrael through the deepe waters of Iorden: where they paſſed on foot, and went dry ſhod to land.

The Iſraelites breaking the couenant of the Lorde their God, & ſtanding in their rebellion were deſtroied out of the land of Iudah, and Ieruſalem, and made ſlaues to the Chaldeans: whereby they were taught by experience (and ſo are wee by the ſame example) what it is to deſpiſe the Lord of hoſtes, and to ſtand in diſobedience againſt his maieſtie.

The Lord reſtoring *Iacob* out of Chaldea to his inheritance againe, according as he had promiſed by the mouthes of his Prophets: doth teach vs by experience

how

The Epistle.

how faithfull he is in his promises, that we therefore should rest vpon him without doubting.

Christ our Sauiour wrought wonders before all Israel, that their eyes might see his diuine power and beleeue him for his works sake: but they beleeued not their owne eyes, and are therefore confounded by the experience that testifieth against their owne consciences.

By examples of experience, the Lord Iesus taught the Iewes, as by that of *Diues* and *Lazarus*, of the sower of seed, of the euill Steward &c. As by familiar demonstrations.

Our forefathers the olde Christians, so polluted their Tabernacles with the workes of impietie, that they extinguished the holy Ghost in the Sanctuarie, whereby they fell to ignorance and corruption, and were giuen ouer to superstition and Idolatrie. The experience whereof should teache vs of these dayes, and our children to walke wisely in the presence of our God.

Experience discouereth the effects of wisdome and folly: and maketh demonstration of the fruits of vertue and of vice, and teacheth to distinguishe, betwixt the righteous and the wicked, betwixt the foole and the wise man, &c.

Experience is the mother and nurse of the policies and gouernements, ciuill and martiall, priuate & publike, guiding the counsailes and doinges of men with orderly discretion.

Experience of the inordinate iniquities of mē suonded the lawes and the iudgement seat.

The experience of the troublesome furies of men

A 3 founded

founded Armes, and aduaunced Militarie profession, for the repressing and restraining of the tyrannies and noyfull malice of the wicked.

The experience of the profit and value of lawe and armes, maketh al prudent states and commonwelths, to embrace and to vphold them both with much care and endeuour.

So to conclude, experience is the ordinarie companion and naturall ornament of reason, which maketh me wise in knowledge, & prudent in the direction and vse of things. He therefore that iudgeth or directeth against experience, is not in deede a man, but a foole more ignorant then a beast.

The experience of other mens harmes, warneth the wise to be ware.

The experience of forren euils, warneth England to waken it selfe out of securitie, and to be watchfull, and wisely to take it selfe.

Experience hath taught me to loue and to honour armes, and in the zeale of a good heart to couet the aduancement of martial occupation, which made me (an vnlettered man) to take vnto me a notarie to sette downe in writing this drift in the defence and praise of warlike prowesse, against al cōtemners of the same: for the benefite and encouragement of my couńtrie & countrimen.

And finally, the experience of the high noblenes & honour of you, my singuler good Lord, doth enboldē me (in the loue of a faithful hart, to your renoumed vertues) most humbly to commend this litle work to your honorable protection, that vnder the shielde of your noble fauour and iudgement, it may stande in grace

grace before our nation, to some good effect. God graunt it. To whom be praise, & to your good Lordshippe, abundaunce of heauenly graces, and fatherly blessings, euen to euerlasting life. Amen. London. 23 Decemb. 1578.

Your honours most humble
GEFFREY GATES.

¶ The defence of Militarie *Profeſsion*.

T hath bene an old controuerſie in the opinions of the Engliſh nation, what profeſſion of life is moſt honorable in worldly ſtates. They being Iſlanders, what by their famous might and proweſſe, and what by the naturall ſafetie of the ſituation of their Soyle,

VVhat worldly eſtate moſt honorable

(enuironed with the maine Ocean ſea, and dwelling in greater ſecuritie, then any one nation that inhabiteth the continent) they may reaſonably differ from the iudgement both of Greekes & Romanes in diſcuſſing this queſtion. For it may well be granted, that the profeſſion and occupation that is moſt in vſe, and moſt neceſſarie for the maintenance and preſeruation of the common wealth, that the ſame ſhould be had moſt in honoure, ſtanding moſt in vſe and value. England therefore dwelling in ſafetie and commonly in peace, may ſeeme to giue the preheminence vnto the lawer: For by his wiſedome and trauel is iuſtice miniſtred, to the maintenance and aduauncement of ſouereigne authoritie: by the benefite of whoſe maieſty, Reuenge

B and

and Tyrannie is forbidden in publique and priuate, euery iniurie and quarell committed to the iudgement and direction of the law: that the vnnaturall rage and furies of ẏ mightie, of the cruel, & of the wicked, being restrained and repressed, sociall vnitie and vniuersall obedience may be nourished and holden in the ciuil fellowship of men: so that the Lambe may sucke safely by the Wolfe, the Calfe by the Leoparde, and the Asse feede quietly by the Lion, &c. And happie is the state where this is accomplished by the industrie and prudence of the peaceable Lawyer. But forasmuch as the thoughtes of man are wicked euen from his youth, and all his wayes naturally inclined to extreme euill, desirous to satisfie his owne lusts and affections with iniurie and crueltie, to reuenge, and to reigne in his owne will and power without correction, and yeldeth not vnto the obedience and direction of any other but for feare of stripes: There must bee therefore an other state and profession of men, whose power and prudence must comprehend the maintenaunce and defence, not onely of the Seate of Iustice, but also of the Cowe and Plowe, of the Bed and Cradle, yea of the Altar and of the souereigne state: which resteth in the profession neither of the Priest nor Lawyer, nor in the occupation of the Housbandmen, Artisans nor Merchants: but lieth in the prowesse and value of them that professe Armes. For when Preaching, processe, Plee, or Perswasion cannot preuaile, in reforming the euils and outrages of the wicked: then must the sword of violence be put in execution, by the hands of them that are able, and skilfull to abase and to extinguish the furies of tumults and Rebellions: and either to bring to obedience the disordered multitude, or else to cut them off from the earth, that peace and ciuill iustice may possesse and rule all the lande, to the restitutiõ and preseruation of domesticall concord and Societie,

[margin: The onely meane to vpholde the seat of Iustice, & all other estates, is the profession of Armes.]

Militarie profession.

Societie, without the which mankinde shoulde decay from the face of the earth, & the rest that remained in the worlde, should be in more miserable state then the wilde beasts of the desert. And as it is proued by experience in all ages, that Iustice and Ciuil pollicie is not surely seated without ye ayde & attendance of Martial gard: So is it to be sene, that where military prowesse hath in any part of the worlde moste preuailed, there hath orderly most flourished, Iustice, Noblenesse, Science and all manner of vertuous and commendable occupations both of body & minde. Witnes of Greece, Italie, and France, and nowe last of Germany. Whereupon this is to be cōcluded, ỹ as Iustice is not of it self able to set vp it selfe in authoritie, and to exercise rule ouer the multitude of Adams rebellious and stiffenecked broode, without the friendship & ayde of Armes: so must wee estéeme martial prowesse, as the common fortresse, wherein ciuill Policie with all her partes and appendants, are hatched, nourished, & preserued: for the orderly nourishment and preseruation of Man and Beast, of Fishe and Foule, of Fire and Salte, of Earth & Water. Where this benefit wanteth, there wanteth Science and gouernement, without which, the whole worlde woulde soone become a desolate wildernesse, & without man to manure or to inhabite it. So that the wickednesse and transgressions of men being the founder and mother of humane lawes and pollicies, we must giue most honourable place to that profession and occupation, that is moste of force and value to chastise the wickednes of the wicked, and to vphold the righteous: to preserue the weaklings & little ones, and to giue frée passage and estimation to right, and vertue. And further, as man naturally is inclined to pride and emulation, and thereby infected with malice and couetousnesse, and looke how much mightier the person is that is possessed of the vices, so muche

VVhere militarie prowesse preuaileth iustice florisheth & al vertues

B. ij.   the

the more hurtfull they are in worke and practise. And therefore are they moste pestiferous and noyfull in kinges and soueraigne Princes, whiche as they are of hautie courage and ambitious, so are they daungerous and commonly full of quarrels & troublesome to their Neighbours. When such are encouraged with a desire to conquer and to bring to their obedience, them that are free from their bondage, or to spoile them of liues, goodes, and habitations: they are not ruled ouer by the equitie of lawe, neither pacified by persuasions nor mollified with praying or preaching, but violence must be resisted with violence, and one lawlesse iniurie satisfied with an other iniurie, which without the force and terror of armes cannot be once offered, much lesse accomplished. Euery state therefore that wanteth the garde and assistance of martial prowesse, lieth open to be ruinated by euery spoiler that will inuade it: whereby we finde that no state, Kingdome, Empire, or common wealth, can stande in any assured safetie, either inward or outward but by the benefite of military profession, the friend and nurse of Lawes, of Religion and of ciuell concord. The necessarie vse and high value whereof made the wise Grecians and valiant Romans, to commend all high courages to the vse and exercise of Armes, as the noblest and most profitable occupation that a worthie minde should desire: whiche estimation it also holdeth continually and must in al estates kingdomes, and Empires of the continent of the world. And though the wickednesse & infidelitie of the world, be generally punished by sworde fire, famine, spoyle, and murther, the ordinary workes of warre, Whereby the Iustice of God is executed vpon the inhabitants of the earth: yet hath the Lord planted, mainteined, and restored, his trueth and religion, by the meanes and assistance of warlike force and policie, and practised his most especiall Sonnes in the knowe-

No state in safety without Militarie profession.

Militarie profession.

knowledge of Armes. For *Abraham* being called to receiue the promise of saluation to the whole worlde, and brought by the Lord his God to dwell in the land of Canaan, had of his owne family and aliance aboue three hundred fighting men, by whose power and courage, he not onely defended himselfe and al his from the spoile and iniuries of the wicked, but also reuenged the wrong done to his neighbours, the Kinges of Sodom and Gomorha, and recouering their goodes from the spoylers, hee restored to euerye man his part that was lost by the ouerthrow. For which famous deede of prowesse, *Melchisedech* the King of Salem blessed *Abraham* and praysed the Lorde God, possesser of heauen & earth in his behalfe. Abraham had syghting men.

    In the value of warlike prowesse, *Simeon* and *Leui*, the Sonnes of *Iacob*, reuenged the violation of their Sister *Dyna*, vpon the sonnes of Sychem. Iacobs sonnes.

    By force of Armes, the Israelites comming out of Egypt, made their way through the Amalekites, & vanquished the Kings of Hesbon and Basan: and possessed their landes, their cities, and their riches: so did they vanquish and destroy the mightie Kings, and inuincible people of Canaan, and possessed their landes, and cities. By Armes their posteritie defended their inheritance, and helde the same: for by Armes the Lorde God vanquished and destroied the enemies of *Iacob*, and therefore is called the Lorde God of hostes. By Armes *Cyrus* conquered Chaldea, and possessed Babylon, giuing libertie to *Israel*: yea, and through his great victories restored Sion and Ierusalem, and the people to their inheritaunce againe. By Armes the Romanes enlarged their Empire ouer many nations, & by vertue of their wisdom and prowesse they brought many barbarous countreis to ciuilitie and prosperitie: For where they gouerned, ther raigned Prudence and Iustice, as ordinary companions to Martiall noblenesse. The Israelites.

Cyrus.

The Romanes.

B 3

By the Armes of rude nations, the Goths, Hunnes, & Vandalles: the Lorde visited the proude Empire of the Romanes, for their pride and tyranny, & confounded it.

By the Armes and prowesse of the Emperour *Constantine* the Lord relieued his church, and restored true religion amongst many nations.

By Armes, *El Enfante de Pelago* recouered the kingdom of Leon, and comforted Spaine, in the daies of cruell afflictions, when all the lande was harrowed and possessed by the Moores and Infidels.

By Armes is the worthy kingdome of France garded and preserued in a State moste honorable: so is Spaine: so are the commonweales and principallities in Italy.

By Armes, the Switzers purchased their freedome, and by Armes they defende and preserue their limits and liberties, to their great fame and benefite.

By Armes hath Germany made her might and prudence knowen to the whole worlde: by Armes they holde the maiestie of the Empire in their power and election: and by their inuincible prowesse, they mayntaine and preserue their states and honours, priuate and publike, and are terrible to the nations rounde about them.

By Armes are the kingdomes of Denmarke and Polonia defended and saued from the power of the cruell Russians and Muscouites.

So is Germany from the powers of the cruell and mighty spoylers of the worlde: the Turkes, Tartarians, Muscouites also, and Russians: and by Armes, they establish peace amongst theselues, and are preserued at home and abroad.

By Armes, *Ferdinando* the king of Spaine seazed into his power the West Indias, and by Armes are the same possessed

Militarie profession. 15

possessed and holden in obedience to the Scepter of Spaine.

By the Armes and prowesse of ciuill princes, are many rude and sauage nations subdued to ciuill gouernement.

The Lorde our God vseth no occupation of men in his workes and proceedings vpon earth, like as he doth Militarie prowesse: For by it hee executeth his wrath and Iustice vpon the rebellious and faithlesse people of the world.

Also by the same meanes it pleaseth the heauenly maiestie to deliuer the righteous from oppression, and to giue waye to his trueth vppon the earth, to restore his Churche, and to defende his Sanctuarie from the rage and violence of the tyrants: As for example.

After the great and wonderfull fauour of God in relieuing and comforting his Church in olde time by the Emperour Constantine, being suffocated with heresies and ruinated by persecutions: the rebellious and bastarde christians, falling from the way of trueth, and abandoning the pathes of righteousnes, were not onely deliuered ouer to the regiment and conduction of Antichrist, and made slaues to the Scepter of darkenesse: but were also for their incurable corruptions in Asia, Greece, and Affrica, deliuered ouer into the power of the cruell Turkes and Sarrasens: whome the Lord raised of a vile people, to be mightie, dreadfull, and inuincible in Armes, for the lamentable spoile, ruine, and extirpation of many Empires, states, kingdomes, & nations, not onely in honour, names, bonds, and liberties: but also in ciuill policies, honest sciences, in knowledge of true religion, and in the verye tongues, generations, and procreations of the vanquished people. Wherein the Lorde hath shewed foorth a fearefull hande of his intollerable wrath and Iustice for the

Constantine by armes restored religion.

Turkes were raysed of a vile people to spoyle the bastard Christians.

sinne

sinne and disobedience of these irrecouerable nations: to the good warning of the nations that doe yet rest in their olde seates, in knowledge eke and libertie to professe and to serue GOD, according to his trueth in Christ Iesus. Which if they abuse and contemne as their forefathers did, and as they of Asia, Africa, and Greece haue also done, and receiued their punishment for their offences by vtter destruction: then let vs and our children looke that the Lord God of hostes (High generall of all warres) can leuie an inuincible Armie, when and where him lysteth, to vexe vs, and to punishe vs, and vtterly to destroy vs. For it is he onely that beareth the sword of vengeance, that striketh in the battell, and giueth the victorye to himselfe. The warre is his, the Armie is his, and he is cheefteyne of the feelde: and as hee vseth them for the punishment of the worlde, so doth he occupie the same also to the comfort and deliueraunce of the righteous, and to make way for the Scepter of peace, (that is, of true religion) to come to her regement and orderly occupation. Wherein the Lord hath shewed and daylie doth more and more shewe, his wonderfull works and power in this last restitution of his Gospel: which began in Germanie with peace, but was forced to holde on the way, by the ayde of warlike prowesse and fidelitie: which was valiantly attempted, and prosperously atchieued by that famous Souldier of God, *Maurice* Duke of Saxoni, the first vanquisher of the Armed enemies of the Gospell in this latter restitution.

  By the fidelitie also and industrie of Militarie occupation, doth the Lord holde possession for his saintes in the proude and mightie kingdome of France, preseruing Rochel the fortresse of his sanctuarie, for the inuocation of his holy name amongst that nation, in true religion.

  That holy citie Geneua with all the godly places

Marginal notes: The victorie is of God. — Maurice. — Rochel. — Geneua.

Militarie profession. 17

of the neighbourhead and confederacie, are also garded by Armes, as the appoynted meanes which God occupieth for the defence of his people, against ye power of their ennemyes. By armes also, hath the Lorde God of hostes entred foot in *Belgia*, and there taught the ignorant hands to fighte, and the slowe couraged, to be bolde and hardie. Whereby the pride of the ennemyes is daunted, and their glorye abased, (and that before oure eyes) in such apparant and wonderfull maner, as wee may wel say that the Lorde of hostes is abrode with his armyes, to pourchase to himselfe honor and prayse, for the yeere of his redemed is come: neither will he geue ouer ye fielde any more, til he hath vtterly destroyd his ennemyes, and confounded the wicked for euermore, and giue perpetuall rest to *Israel*, accordyng as it is writen. Warre in Belgia.

Thes being the publique effects and workes of martiall Industrie: what occupation or vocation darre putte forth it selfe to make comparison with it? the exercise and substance whereof consisteth of prudence, high courage, and magnamitie. Prudence, to inuent, to direct, and to gouerne. Courage, to execut and to perfourme that which politique prudence hath deuised and set downe to be done. And magnanimitie, to sustayn with irremoueable temperancye what soeuer happeneth. And farther to amplifie vpon the praise of this occupation, what worke or volume can be sufficient to expresse in orderly recital the noblenesse and particular vertues of the famose martialistes of the olde and later worlde, which stande renoumed in hystories: and for euery one left to memory by name, a thousand of great worthines are past ouer without mentione. But this is generally to be noted in the warlike Princes and Nobilitie: that as they exceede in militarie prowesse and worthines, so doe they excell in wisedome and all noblenesse of hart: Whereof warlike industrie consisteth

Warlike Princes.

C.i.

hart: and hee that will worthely bee called a militarie man, must cast off all vilanies and basenes of minde: and full charge his thoughtes and doinges with honeste inclinationes and like effectes. Neither are the commendable vertues of the minde so necessarye for any occupatione, as they are for them that professe and exercise armes. And the martialist that wanteth them, shall not prosper in warre, but sinke in obloquie and dishonor: neither is there anye state or vocation of man that can worse susteyne, the infection and vse of vices, then can an army gouerned in warlike maner. Foolishe therefore and beastely is the common speach, vsed of the base and humble mynded sort of our natione, that doe not onely saye, but also affirme in their doinges, that the worst sort of men, (and such as for the vilenes of their conditiones the earth is not able to susteyne) are fit for the warres: and accordingly doe call out the refuse of the people to be soldiers for the seruice of their Prince and countreie, where in deede the worthiest people ought to be chosen, and preferred: as to a state most honorable, and of most credite and importance.

Commendable vertues necessarie for them that professe Armes.

But if Englande stood in the continent of the world enuironed with mightie nationes, that in the dayes of frendeship would moue discretion to feare their malice in the time of controuersy: then should it know ye value of a soldier, & lick the dust off the feete of her men of prowesse: then would the lawer & the marcheant humble themselues to the warriers, & be glad to geue honour & salary to the martialist: and shew frendly grace to his page, and fauor to his lackye. And al be it our state is better at ease and that we by the benefite of the seate of our lande, doe stande in more securitie then the nations of the firme land: yet is not our assurance such as may so deliuer vs vp in the time of peace, to ye carelesse & spitefull contempt of armes: as though the common

Militarie profession.

mon welth and ſtate publique ſtoud in ſuch proſperitie and ſaftie, by the wiſedome of the lawier and by the riches of the marchant, as that they ſhould neuer ſtande in neede of militarie forces, nor to nouriſhe men of warre, but to conſume them with penurye and with the galowes. Let al the miſerable drudges of this preſent worlde, (whoſe God is their belly, and whoſe idoll is their riches) that ſo beaſtly and oprobriouſly diſdaine the warlik people, looke into the recordes not onely of the former times of olde, but alſo of theſe preſent dayes, and ſee in what hazarde, not onely the Throne of their ſouereigne Prince, but alſo the whole ſtate of the common welth (and conſequently, the cheſt, the chamber, the bedde, and cradle, the wife and daughter of the lawier and marchant, the Pulpyt, and Preacher, the Iudge and the Iudgement ſeat) haue bene to ſuffer generall and particuler ſhipwracke, by the conſpiracies, mutinies, and tumultes, of traitors and of the rebellions multitudes of the vulgare people, cruel and implacable: And confeſſe by whoſe diligence, wiſedome, perill, induſtrie and bloud, all theſe thinges haue bene defended, and ſaued out of the power of the furious ſpoylers, reſtoringe iuſtice to her ſeate, the plowe to the feelde, the cowe to the payle, the ſhephearde to his flocke, the merchant to his trade, and the learned to his quiet ſtudy and exerciſe. Yea and let them be aſhamed of their ignobilitie of harts, & conſent with other nationes to geue vnto the people of proweſſe, and militarie profeſſion, the honor that is due vnto them. For it is a rare age of the worlde, wherein the ſureſte kingdome, and the ſafeſte ſtate and nation vpon earth, flieth not at one time or other to the couert and ſuccor of Armes, to ſaue it ſelfe either from inteſtine violence, or from forren depopulation, or elſe from both.

  Whoeſoeuer therefore will ſee the value of martial

The glorious effects of Militarie induſtrie.

C.2.

The defence of

martial prowesse in preseruing a kingdome, in vpholdinge the souereigne maiestie of theire Prince, in redeming their countrie from the power of forren ennemyes mightie and warlike, in pacifyinge ciuil vprores, and in extinguishinge the most ragiouse furies of any rebelles in the worlde: and in reducinge the gouernement to obedience, iustice, housbandry, traffique, literal exercise, and all ciuill policies and ordinances to their places againe. Looke throughe the state of France, from the beginning euen to this day: But specially in the dayes of Kinge *Iohn*, of his sonne also Kinge *Charles* the fift, and eke of *Charles* the sixte, aud aboue all in the dayes of *Charles* the seuenth, who being so molested, and ruinated not onely by the victorious warres of the Englishmen and Bourgonyons: but also by intestin diuisiones & ciuill vprores, that hee helde not the fifte parte of his kingdome in obedience, insomuch that he was driuen to holde himselfe in a smale corner of his lande, and was contempteously called King of Bourges: For his ennemies possessed & ranged al the parts else of his Realme at their pleasures. But that famous King (aided with the prowesse & fidelity of his approued martialistes:) neuer gaue ouer the fielde til hee recouered his kingdome and restored the common welth: which had bene so spoiled, wasted, and depopulat, that the fieldes and vineiards were growen to a wildernesse, their cities become heapes, and their habitationes desolate.

Valiant Kinges in France.

Peace and idlenesse before conquests.

When the Lord meaneth to plague a wicked natione for sinne and to translate them to the power and scepter of another nation: then he filleth them with the fatnesse of the earth, and geeueth them peace that they may wax rotten in idlenesse, and become of dulle wittes, slowe of courage, weake handed, and feeble kneede: that when the spoiler commeth, they may in al pointes be vnfurnished of warlike prowesse, and not

Militarie profession. 21

not able to resiste, but so made a praye to their ennemies. As the Persians were to *Alexander*, the Greekes and Hungarians with many other natones to the Turkes: and the olde Brutes to the Saxons.

And likewise when the Lord meaneth to aduance a nation and to make any people famous and honorable vpon earth: he stirreth them vp to high courage, and maketh their mindes and bodyes apt to the warre, and in all points sufficient for the pursuite and accomplishment of Militarie trauaile. As he did the Israelites for ye recouery of their promised inheritance, by subduing and destroying the mightye Canaanites. *Cyrus* the Persians for the subuerting of ye empire of Syria: *Alexander* the Grecians for the conquering of the Persians, & for translating of the Monarchie from Asia to Europa. The Romanes eke being a poore smale people, and of an opprobrious foundation, were made fit in pollicy and courage for the pursuite and exercise of Armes: whereby they became Lords and commanders of al the chiefe nations, Empires, states, and kingdomes of the world. And againe, for the chastisement and confusion of them the Lord raysed vp to Armes and warlike courage, the rude and barbarous multitudes of the Goths, Hunnes and Vandales. And so the Turkes of a small people, and of the sauage Scythian kinde, to be the most cruell and noyfull spoylers and destroyers that euer were vpon earth, to subuert all ye ciuill states and Empires of Asia and Affrica, and to subdue and depopulat the noble Empire of Greece and the kingdom of Hungarie. Tamberlan a heardman with the rude Scythians to chastise *Baiezet* the Turkish Emperour and all his dominions. And lastly the Spanyard to chastise France, Italy, Germany and lowe Duchland. And now let vs farther beholde with discretion what worke the Lord is entred into by Armes, in these last dayes of the world: And how martiall prowesse and industrie hath mightely

Marginalia: God maketh apt to warre, whome he will aduaunce. — Cyrus and Alexander — Romanes — Goths, &c — Turkes. — Tamberlan. — Spanyards

C.iii. serued

serued to aduaunce the name and glorye of God, and to giue passage to his Gospell, where it lay prostrate and troden vnder the feete of Antichrist and his consorts. For when the time was come, in the yere of our Sauiour Christ 1517. that ye Lord set foote on earth to restore his Sanctuary, he beganne his businesse by a poore ministrie vnder the couert & protection of the most worthie prince Duke *Frederick* of Saxonie, and so encreased vnder the defence of the most noble Princes, *Iohn* Duke of Saxonie, & *Philipe* Lantgraue of Hesse, & of the famous and warlike cities, Augsborough, Strasborough, Vlmes Magdeborough, &c. And when the champions of the kingdome of darkenesse (vnder the conducte of the most renowmed Emperour *Charles* the fifth) seemed to renge the hoste of Israel vnder a terrible victory: then did the Lorde of hostes bestirre himselfe, and frustrating the counsailes, and dispersing the forces of his enemies, he vanquished the troupes of the Philistims by the Armed hand of his chosen captaine *Maurice* Duke of Saxoni: who by the vertue of Martiall prowesse ayded by the Lord God of hostes, brake the teeth of the vngodly, and restored the worde of God to a free passage throughout all Germanie. So did the Lorde preuaile by Armes in Surike: by vertue of which also, wydened the passage of his gospell into France, and by the force and power of one poore towne, there holdeth possession for his Sanctuarie, maugre the might and malice of all his enemies. This being the most glorious effects of Militarie industrie in these saide countreis, to the enlarging of Christes kingdome for the saluation of many, and comfort of the whole worlde: praise the inuincible Arme of our God mighty and victorious in battell: and see yet a greater worke then all these, nowe a doing by force of Armes for the ciuill libertye, and for the freedome of true Religion in lowe Dutchelande: where the hande of the Lorde hath bene so apparant fauourable,

that

The worthie actes of the Duke of Saxoni, Lantgraue &c.

that in all the progresse and successe of these warres it may be saide: This is the worke of the Lord our God, in the sight of all the Heathen, and it is marueilous in our eyes. Let vs therfore examin some part of those affaires, & see how *Iacob* hath preuailed in his warres by slow and vnexpert souldiers, against the most famous, arrogant, & implacable enemies of the gospel of Christ: and then let the swinish fooles that contemne martiall profession, stoppe their mouthes and be ashamed. For the heauens doe reioyce, the worlde is comforted, and *Israel* shalbe glad through ye victories of God, purchased by the fidelitie & prowesse of his valiant men at armes.

When King *Philip* had wearied his good subiects of low Duchland, with fained pacifications, in the aduantage wherof the defendants being taken vnprouided & vnarmed, were daylie spoyled and murthered, they fell to armes for publike defence, & stoode vpon their gard: but béeing ouercome by the false promises of the faithlesse Regent, the Duches of Parma, they accepted conditions of agreement, and while they rested vpon the same, came the Duke of Alua accompanied with chosen forces, and tooke the countrey in charge, as Lieutenant to the King. He planted his bands of warre in all the stronge townes and holdes through out the Lowe countrey: he apprehended the Counties of Horne, and Degremont, and executed them as captains and chiefe pillers of the Mutiners. He builded the Castell of Antwerp for mastering of that proude citie, and renged all the whole Lande vnder feare and oppression, minding to bring the people vnder extreeme exactions, for the nourishment of their own plagues & seruitude: I mean for the maintenāce of the kings forces & fortifications throughout, for the holding of the people in subiection to what yoke or ordinances so euer should be enforced vppon them: Wherein the Duke missed the Tracte of that wisedome and pollycie that was famed to bée

Philip, vexed lowe Duchland

The duke of Alua his force.

in him. For this tirannous porpose coming to common apparance, then reuolted the Holanders and Zelanders, in an vnlikely state to stande to theire cause. But the Lord God of hostes that had stirred vp this quarel, meaning to proue the force of his blowe by an vnlikly host, against the troopes of the prowde and dredfull warriers his ennemyes,) did shewe himselfe sufficient, able to confounde the mightie by the weake, the prudent by the foolishe, the industrious by the slowe, the courageouse by the cowarde, y glorious by the vile, the noble by the churle, and the King by the vassale, the rich and imperiall by the poore and seruile multitude: For comparison beinge consideratly made of the Holanders and rude Zelanders with their King: hee mightie in powers both by lande and by sea, standinge in continual redines: they weak and vnprouided both for lande and water: he in renowmed armes, stronge, experimented, and politique: they naked, and of al other their Kings people and subiects, contemned for their natural slowenes, cowardise, ignorance, dronkenesse, and most vnwarlike spirites: the King infinite in artillarye, munitiones, treasures, and eke in frends, lieutenantes, commanders, & martiall bands of incomparable fame and approued value: the mutiners easye to be exhausted of their monie, vnfurnished of all habilementes of warre, of trained Soldiers, and experimented Capteines, and hauinge their neerest neighbours, yea and them of their kinred and alience, to bee their moste fyerse and noifull enemies. And in this vnequal match to entre warre, it woulde haue seemed a motion in the mutiners, proceedinge rather of a desperat rage, then grounded vpon any reasonable hope to preuaile to any other effect, then to the thraldome and confusion of themselues, and of their posteritie. Howe be it the Lord that commandeth his Soldiers, and capteines that beare armes in the quarell of trueth

God by an vnlikely hoste sheweth his might

Hollanders and zelanders against Philippe King of Spaine.

Militarie profession.   25

trueth and righteousnesse, not to feare the multitude of their enemies: stode by the Hollanders in their honest cause, and hath iustified their quarell, & wil maintaine it to the ende, as it seemeth at this day. For hee hath in the behalfe of that contemned people (nay rather to make good the glory of his great name against the vanity of flesh & blood) brought impossible thinges to a marueilous prooffe: Els coulde it not haue come to passe, that poore litle and weake Vlushing, shoulde haue famished and subdued the riche, large, and strong Citie of Middlebourgh, aided by the riche and mightie townes of Antwerpe and Ansterdam, and eke of Tregose, and Barowe: and garded with 2000. approoued Souldiers, vnder the commaundement of that famous Gentleman, *Mont Darragon*, who was driuen by distresse of victuals (all the forces of the king being not able either to relieue him or to succour him) to render vp the town, departing from it with 1400 men of war in armes: wherby the whole Island of Walkeren came entirely vnder the direction of the Prince of Orange, to the inspeakeable comfort of the cause publike. For by the benefite of this victory, ye Zelanders, vtterly vanquished the kinges forces vppon the Sea and bet him quite from it: whereby the Brabanders and Flemings, were put from their fishing and traffike, other then vnder the courtesie of the Zelanders: which so endamaged all the continent of the lowe countrey, that the inhabitaunts finding themselues pressed in an extreeme wrenche, betwixt the warres of their neighbours, and the oppression of the Spanyardes: they fell in conclusion to ioyne handes with the mutiners, in a more conuenient and a farre better policie, and in a more assured hope, that by a generall consent in Armes, they might redeme their countrey frō the power of ye oppressers, and driue the Spanyards with their adherents out of the lande: then to nourish the warres against their

marginal notes: Litle Vlushing famished strong Middleborough.

The lowe countrie reuolted from the Spanyards

D   neigh-

neighbours, in whose discomfiture and subuersion stood the thraldome of them all: in whose victorie, the libertie and desired restitution of the one and of the other should rest assured. Herevpon proceeded the generall reuolt of all the lowe cuntrie, yea rather enforced by the good successe and prowesse of the Hollanders and Zelanders, then willingly accepted of them of Flanders, Brabant, and of other Countries, for anye free zeale to the cause publike. But blinde were the heartes of them that did not see, that the Prince of Orange and his poore vnexperimented adherents, were the very Army of the Lord God of hostes, who will neuer faile to breake the Iawes of his aduersaries, turning their wisedome to folly, and their glory to shame: which was fully accomplished in the Duke of Alua, that dreadfull and renowmed chieftaine of the Papistes. For had not hee bene ouercome with a very tirannous madnes, hee woulde not haue entred his gouernement in Belgia with oppression, murther, pillage, and intollerable decrees, vpon the people that were (by easier prouocations then these, stirred and ready to breake out in Armes) in mind rather to dye in the field for the defence of their ancient liberties (so dearly purchased and defended by the blood of their forefathers) then to yeeld themselues and their posteritie vnder the heauie yoke, and arrogant domination of so implacable people, as bee the Spanyardes: which might well haue bene considered in the wisdome of the Duke of Alua, but that God blinded him with the might of his Prince, and the opinion of himselfe, that if this whole Countrie of lowe Ducheland, should in generall consent fall to Armes, and withstand their Prince by vyolence, and that they were not to bee reduced to obedience, but by extreeme warres, and infinit charges: after much blood and spoyle of the lande, the King should reduce them to his yoke and subiection by the sworde: that euen so, and by that wearisome and

The good successe of the Hollanders and zelanders, caused the rest of the countries to ioyne with them

cruell

cruell meanes, he must euer after reteine them & their posterity in his obedience: which would be an intollerable charge to him, and would set downe a continuall pillage and oppression vppon the Subiectes: whereof should ensue the orderly decaye of the common wealth, and nourishe a perpetuall malice in the people against their Soueraigne Lorde, and continually pricke them to tumultes: which at the last, shoulde eyther set them free and reiect their Prince, or els vtterly confounde them by the increase of their tyrannie and miserable seruitude, which also would eate the king out of his inheritance. But had the Duke called to memorie howe apt this nation hath bene in olde time to fall to warre in quarell of their liberties, and for defence of their ancient compositions: and how they shooke of the tyrannous Soueraigntie of the French kings (yet more gentle and profitable then this of the Spanyards) and howe dearely and painefully the French kings haue in times past forced their obedience, and coulde not, but were at the last, after much warres and many bloody victories, quite shut out: he would haue endeuoured his wisdome and labour to reconcile them by mollifying the gouernment, and by gratious gentlenes and bountie, rather then proudlye to presse downe the yoke that had already wearied them: which cannot prosper, nor long endure: for the Lord God in his Iustice hateth tyrannie, and destroyeth tyrants from the face of the earth: and vsually destroyeth the roote and branche of euerye cruell grinder of the faces of the poore, and casteth him of for euermore. *Tyranny abhored of God & man.*

 And farther, he fell into this ouersight: that he exceeded so farre in the proportion of the kings charges, by fortifications, and superfluous supplies: aboue all the leuie and receiptes that were to come in, by all the pillage, dueties, and lones that he could deuise: that he ranne indebted to the men of warre, aboue xxxiij. Monethes

nethes paye, whereby the souldiers became disordered spoylers: & at the last so mutinous, that the Spanyardes forced their pay, and bound the Duke to shamefull conditions, and for his last farewel he was forced to kéepe his lodging vnder gard, & durst not present himselfe openly to the men of war at his departure out of Belgia, vntil the Commander *Don Lewes de Requezes* the new lieutenant, had giuen his promise, in the wordes of the king, and set downe an order for the soldiers full pay.

With these errors he ioyned many faultes in the direction & pursuit of these wars: which turned to the aduauntage of the poore defendauntes, but much to the disgrace & discredit of himself. Immediatly vpõ the getting of Harlam, & the horrible massacher there done: the Spanyards mutined for their pay: & putting away their cõmanders & officers of sworn loyalty, they chose vnto thẽselues a coronel, captains, & other officers, & at the opening of the day, they toke vp their ensigns & marched toward the wals of Harlam, & making vpon them that garded the vnrepaired breaches of the same, they draue thẽ to abandon their charge, & folowed thẽ with match in the cock into ye market place: & there *Monseur Lamot* & *don Iulius Rhomero* (who with fiue ensignes of footmen possessed & garded the town) being assembled with their companies, departed with their people, leauing ye town to the possession of the mutiners: which standing stiffely vpon the demand of their ful paye, & finding the Duke slow & ouersterne to yeelde to the same, they fained that they would kéepe the towne to the vse of the States of Holland, & the prince of Orange: & that they would surrender it to *Monseur Delorge:* which brought the Duke into such a perplexitie, that hee passed conditions with the mutiners: such as danted his glory and hautinesse, more then any one matter that euer happened to him in all his life.

Thus was he impeched, and could not, neither did he seeme

marginal note: The siege of Harlam

Militarie profession. 29

seeme to be desirous to folowe the opportunitie that ỹ victorie ouer Harlam did present, to the great aduancement of his seruice, had he folowed it with like industry & expedition: For the terror of that atchiuement, & eke of the ouerthrowe of the countey Batenburgh with the Princes armie, had opened vnto him al the Gates in Holland, had he hotly pursued the aduantage geuen.

After he had reconciled the mutiners, & set al things in order in Harlam, hee went forth to beset Alkemer: where he arriued vpon ỹ day of a great faire holden in the towne: which was therefor filled with the countrey people yong & old, & with catle, without garde of men of warre, without store of victuales, or of any other habilements of warr: sauing ỹ Captein *Richauer* through great perill & industrie entred ỹ towne with 500. men of warre. The Duke battered ỹ towne in soundry places, & assaulted it fearcely, & was repulsed: he cōmanded the seconde assault, & as ỹ Spaniards made towarde the wall, there fel a very terrible tēpest of haile rain wind and thunder, that so danted & the Souldiers, that refusing the seruice they turned vpō their Commanders, and would not forwarde: for the former attempts were deerely bought. The Duke seeing the Capteins to sley their own souldiers for their disobedience, commanded retrait, and so ỹ assailants returned to their lodgings, minding to gather better courage against ỹ next day: But the tempest continewed al that night, and powred down such aboundance of raine, ỹ by ỹ morning, their cheef enchamping ground was al vnder water, & most of the peeces that battered, lay suncken vp to the axiltree, & for the softnes of the ground might not then by no meanes be recouered. Wherevpō ỹ Duke dislodged himself, & encamped farther frō ỹ towne in a dry soile, from whence also within a few days he remoued quite away, after that hee had spente full sixe weekes in that siege to his great losse & dishonor: for by that day that

The duke of Alua by a tempest driuen from the seege of Alkemer.

D.3.   he

hee gaue it ouer, the Towne was not victualled for sixe dayes.

This was the Dukes last attempt in Holland, and this his repulse much hardened & encouraged the Hollanders to stande fast in their cause.

<small>The duke of Alua vnto his last trump</small> Hee had so farre exhausted the kings Treasure and his owne money, that he borowed.12000.gylderns of his host in Amsterdam, to bear his charges into Spaine. Thus this great Duke that came into Belgia so glorious and dreadful, is daunted & returned into Spaine with shame and discredite.

Then succeded in his charge, *Don Lewes de Requezes* greate Comander of Castile: who practising to mingle hypocrisie and bloud in one drift and policie, (that was to snare and to confounde the Prince of Orange) hee preuailed in both lesse then he hoped. For he could no more preuaile against Israel, then did *Fernando de Toledo*. Duringe his gouernement, was the kinges nauey and all his forces by sea quite vanquished and broken. First as they relieued Midleburgh by Estecaple vnder the conduct of S. de Beuoys: in which exploit perished viii.or ix.shippes great and small.

At the conflict by Rhomers wall, the Papistes making forth to the fight, vnder the gouernement of *Iulius Rhomero:* they were discomfited with the losse of xvi.or xvii.boates of warre,& aboue 1500.of their most chosen Soldiers: where that valeant *Iulius* flyinge the terror of the Zelanders, hardely saued his life, recouering to lande by a Scute, where also the Commander stode lokinge on the fight with a crosse in his hande, and a Frier at the right side of him, prayinge together for the good successe of the batell: wherein it appered that the Lorde hearde them not, yet were the Zelanders sore spente and weakened, with ix. weekes colde wynter lyinge on shippeborde, thinnely clothed, & as thinnely dieted, with browne bread, cheese, redde heringes and smal small beere, in all poyntes inferiour to their enemies: but God was with ye poore, against the prowde and mightie: to him be the glorie and the praise.

Upon Whitsondaye next folowinge, ye Zelanders invaded & spoiled the rest of the Kings nauey in the riuer of Andwerpe. The Papistes once beseeged the citie of Leyden for the space of sixe monethes, and preuailing not, they departed. Nowe being enformed that the Towne was vnfurnished of men of warre, and none woulde receiue, and vnstored of victualles and none would prouide, but reiected the commandement of the Prince in both these pointes, they come agayne, and shut vp the vnarmed city with such forces, that the prince and states were not able to make any resonable attempte to succor the distressed Towne by land: which made them to fal in deuise to drowne the countrie, preparinge an Armada, of small boates wel appoynted for the purpose: whiche after dificult passage on the moste part of their way, were stalled at Sonterwold xi. dayes in wanne hope for want of water to carie the through their appointed voyage. The Admiral Boysot hauinge one day dispatched a post to the Prince lying at Delft, with letters to certifie his exellencie of the vntowardnesse of their attempt: the beseged in that while, destitute of al maner of victuals, were in an inclination to talke for compositiones with the ennemye. But the Lorde that woulde bring them to vnderstande howe much he was on their side, and euer at hand with them that faithfully truste in him, in the same very night next folowinge the saide dispatch of the post with the Admirals comfortelesse letters to the Prince, & when that all their councelles were shutte vp in a hopelesse dungel, came a mightie wynde from the Northe West, which draue the Ocean sea to runne in at the sluces & breaches of the sea walles so violently, that in the drift of one tide, the water was flowed vp three foote and a halfe

The Lord prouideth for the zelanders contrary to expectation.

halfe deepe, where it was not a shaftment deepe, at the dispatch of the saide post. Then did the Admirall so besturre him, that he the next forenoone dislodged them of the first scoute, & so them of Leiden Dam, and of Leiden Dorp: and so terrified all the ennemies dispersed in scouts, to the number of 12000. men of warre, that they ranne away from all their standinges, and abandoned the siege, in a flyinge feare. And the Admiral poursuinge the occasion with great industry and courage, arriued with his shallowe and vitorious nauie at the walles of the hungrie Towne. And forthwith sent aduertisements to the Prince of this most happie and vnlooked successe, within xxiiii. howres of the former contrary letteres. And this was a wonderfull worke of God, by the hands of a people, earst slowe, feareful and vnwarrelike: and nowe (by the exercise of Armes, and conduct of the General commander of all Armies) industrious, hardye, and vanquishers of the most warrelike. Here is to be noted for a wonderful worke of God also. In the verie nighte that the winde so serued the point, to driue the flodde ouer the lande, 200. pases of the wales of the besieged Citie fel into the ditch, with such a noise as terrified ÿ ennemies, as it had bene the noise and sturre of the aduersaries cominge in a Camisado, whiche made the Papistes to flie their places, to the discomfiture of all them that were in the farther scoutes, assaulted by the Admiral and his people, and so ranne all away without any resonable cause why, other then the feare that God strake in their hartes. God also prouided further for the miraculous preseruation of that Towne: that where at the first pitchinge of the siege, they made proportion of their victualles but for two monethes, accordinge to the nomber within: the Lord sent a plague that diminished of thē six thousand and more: and so leauing not aboue seuen hundreth able men to weare Armes, the victuals serued for sixe monethes:

Militarie profession. 33

monethes: but xv. dayes before the succours came, they were vniuersally without bread within the towne, & two or three dayes without any maner of foode: yet were not ye faithfull & valeant Bourgars weery of their partes: so deere is ciuil libertie, and so terrible & odious is irksome seruitude and oppression to honest & manly hartes. Then folowed, the surprise of Schonehouen, Olderkyrk. &c. by the Papistes: and inuadinge also the Ilande of Zeland called Scowen, where at their entry, perished ye noble and faithful gentleman *Charles Boysot* Generall gouernor for the Prince in Zeland, being hurt with the shotte of one of his owne people. They besieged Bomenyer, a litle village fortified at the sodeyne by the countrie men, who had to their aide and defence of the place, Capteyne *Hooke* and two hundreth Germanes, whoe together with the valiant Boores (newely made martialists) so approued their prowesse and fidelitie, that they all (sauing fiue men) spent their liues in resistinge the fierse assaultes of the ennemies, which at the sixth assault recouered the place, where many a worthie Soldier of the Spanyardes perished, to the number of 3000. and vpwardes: amonge whiche were some such speciall Capteines and Gentelmen, as the losse of them brake the very hart of the famous *Marques Vittello*, wherevpon the Commander made a vowe, that he woulde neuer more attempt to winne towne in Hollande or Zelande by force of assault.

Zurickesea being also surprised by the Papistes (a towne full of corrupt Papistes, & common whores) the Hollanders and Zelanders began to doubt of their matters: and greatly to feare the forewardenesse and successe of their ennemies: and distrusting their owne state and value, they laboured for to obteine aide and confederacie abroad: where they founde such colde comfort, that they might well say. *Non est Salus in filijs hominum*. Whilest they stode yet reeling and coulde

Zuriksea surprised, by the Papistes.

not

The defence of

not finde a sure grounde to rest vpon, the Lorde that in this maner doth vse to trie ye faith of his people (and findeth litle in fleshe and bloude but feare and distrust in God) awakened, and wrought for himselfe: and at a moment altered so the state of thinges that the Commander being dead, the Duke of Arskot, the countie Meusfeelde and Monseur Barliamount, entred the Gouernement ciuil and martial, vntil the King sent thither the Lorde *Iohn of Austria*: who at his first comming behaued himselfe so sweetely, that hee woulde seeme of faithfull intent and deuior to reduce the common welth to peace, concord, and obedience, by gentlenes & liberal dealing: and vpon this deuise, passed couenantes of reconciliation through al: for the credite & accomplishement whereof, he forced himselfe to swarue from al reasonable policies, in drawinge the Spanyardes and the bands of warr out of the strong places, in abandoning the Castle of Andwerp, in remouinge the Kings forces out of al the lowe countrie, in executinge certeine Spanyardes, in concluding himselfe to doe nothing without the consent of the States, in the gouernement ciuil or martial, in ratifying the pacification of Gannt: In all which drifts he ment to illude the States, and to dare the Prince of Orange (as a lark) til he had snared them al in his power, and then to execute his bloudy intention: whiche the Lorde God frustrated, turning this wise platte of the Papistes, to the vtter ouerthrowe of theire porpose, and to the euerlasting shame and discredite of the Lorde *Iohn*: who by this fondly fette deuise, shutte himselfe out of all, and dying vanquished by his owne foly and slowenes, he is for euer shrowded with this opinion amongest wise men, that hee was verye voide of depe policies, of martial prowesse, and eke of militarie industrie, and so let him rest with *Don Lewys*. Their bosting pride and malice is at an end, & the Lord God of hostes procedeth in his warres, and so shall hee

The duke of Austria his fonde & false deuise failed him.

confounde

Militarie profession.   35

confounde and consume al his ennemyes from the face of the erth: prosper and aduance his name, his trueth, and glorie, and make the Crowne of his anointed to florish, by the hands of his men of prowesse, and by the value of his armed martialistes, by whose labour and industrie he hath wrought and done al thes thinges before our eyes, and wee behold them euen in our bedes. Praise God therefore, and geue honor to his faithfull Souldiers: & let the coueteous merchant, and the ambitious lawier leaue of his drudgerie for greedy lucre, despise the delicacie of his belly, & dassh ye wantonnes of his eyes, and cast his idol out of his seruil hart: that is, senseles auarice, and put on Armes, & furnishe himselfe with policie and warlike Prowesse, yf hee will iustely be numbred amongst the people of noblenesse & honor.

Hauinge said somewhat concerning militarie profession and militarie men in general, nowe behoueth it to describe what kinde of man is worthy of the name of a martialist, what men did proffesse and exercise this occupation in old time, now doe, and hereafter must: and eke to distinguishe betwixt Souldier and Souldier: *The qualities of militarie men.* that the profession in his selfe nature and qualitie may stand vnattaynted before the malignant & foolishe aduersary, & walke freely deliuered from the scourse and corruptions of ye lewd multitude ye vante themselues of Souldiership, that throgh their vilenes, doe geue matter to the rotten & idle bellies to depraue, & so to despise martial Armes, that in their seruile discretion they iudge it a discredite for an honest man to be a souldier. ⸿ The man that loueth right and honoreth iustice, is fit to be ye defendor of the same: he ye is merciful to ye pore, and pitieth the afflicted, is a meete man to succour his countrie nation & against the violence of tirantes and oppressors: he that loueth the habitationes of the iust, & the prosperity of ye righteons: he ye tendereth ye widowe and the fatherles; he that delighteth to se science, social

C.2.   amitie,

Who is to be accompted a right souldier.

amitie, and vertue to flourishe in his countrie, deuine honor aduanced, faith, peace, and equitie to reigne in euerye felowshippe, and hateth couetousnes, robbery, theft, extortion, brawlinges, striffe, murther, fornication, idlenesse and dronkenesse, that man is worthie and fit to be a Soldier. For the first foundation and vse of Armes was erected of necessitie, to restreine and to represse the violent crueltie, and beastly disorder of men, and to establishe social peace and Iustice vppon earth: which els coulde haue had neither seat nor possession in the worlde, for that the nature of man is so euel, and his hart so peruerse that there is no meane to bridle his furies, and to hold him any while in a peaceable order, but by feare of corporal punishement. For howe vnwillinge man is naturally to bee subiecte to the rule and direction of an other, and to suffer an examiner of his offenses, and to minister stripes for the same, that woteth euery hart of flesshe in his owne feeling and vnderstandinge. The power therefore and wisedom, to reforme & to gouern people is absolutly giuen of God, for the benefite and preseruation of mankinde, established & vpholden by force of Armes, as the mean, iudged fittest in the heauenely wisdome, to preserue and to gouerne this rude and rebellious worlde.

The cheefe man therefore of militarie order, is ech souereigne prince in his state & gouernement. Hee being a man complet in all the vertues & condicions that are behoofull to one of that charge and professsion: shall passe full fraighted of loue & honor, and rest in glorie & prayse vpon earth, as the Sunne in the firmament.

The office & charge of euery soueriegne maiestie in general, is to minister iustice, for the maintenance of right and domesticall peace amongest his people, & eke to defende the same from intestine and forren violence. For the true accomplishement whereof, this Prince or cheefteine, must be furnished with prudence to
consider

consider the state and nature of all partes and particulars pertaining to the commodity and aduauncement of the health and wealth of his people, priuate, and publike: and accordingly to prouide to establishe and to continue the same.

For as hee is the heade of his people, so must he bee their wisdom, their light, and their example: and looke what equitie, what modestie, what temperance, what vse and exercises of vertue he would should raigne and dwell in his people, of the same must hee himselfe bee the very springing Fountaine, running in continuall streames throughout all his Regiment: *In vulgus enim manant exempla regentum.* The Commons doe followe, as they haue their ruler for a guide. But seeing that corruption doth sticke so fast in flesh and blood, that neither Prince nor vassall can be without imperfections: we must allowe more libertie of infirmities, in the citie then in the fielde. *The prince should be an example to his people.*

For as the Armed hoste is the extreeme remedie to chastise, and to represse the insolencie, iniuries, and offences of others, so shoulde the regiment of warre be free from the same: & euery vice in a Souldier strongly bridled and extremely punished. So did and doe all Cheiftaines that euer preuailed, or shall preuaile by Armes, and be renowmed in Militarie prowesse. For where corruption and libertie is suffered in a Souldier, there is the shame and confusion of Armes. Precise Discipline therefore, is the ordinarie nourse of honorable warfare: whereby the Prouerbe (no lesse wise then it is olde) is also profitable, as it is moste true, He that is fitte for the Chappell, is meete for the fielde. And whereas Armes are most in vse and bee best gouerned, there are the vertues and worthinesse of the minde had most in exercise and honour. Whereof it followeth, that the Cheeftaine must be wise in counsaile, temperate in life, affable in speach, faythful in words, *Vices in soldiers must strogly be bridled.*

E 3   courteous

courteous in greeting, wakefull in charge, prouident in perill, abstinent in dyet, continent in life, apt to traueile, prudent and couragious in Battell, constant in wisdome, prowesse, and vertue: bountifull to the worthie, amiable to the honest, seuere to the wicked, gratious to the afflicted, and mercifull to the Captiue, modest in victorie, and constant in magnanimitie, not fearing the frailetie of warlike state and prosperitie, nor drowping vnder the alteration of the same: Such a prince is a compleat Martialist. Such was *Iupiter Belus*, that first repressed by force of Armes, the furious crueltie, and ragious insolencie of men, and subdued many people to the authoritie of ciuill gouernement, laying thereby the foundation of the Empire of Syria: whereof proceeded such a benefite to mankinde, that he was esteemed and honoured as a soueraigne God amongst the Gentils. So was *Hercules* of Lybia, that for to chastise the tyrannous *Girones* that vsurped and oppressed Spaine, toke his voyage out of his countrie into Spaine and destroied them: And after his returne, came *Cacus* out of Italie and molested Spaine, which brought *Hercules* againe: who vanquishing the robber, redeemed the land and people, restoring them to ciuill peace and libertie: whereby he purchased deuine honour amongst the heathen.

<small>Iupiter Belus:</small>

<small>Hercules.</small>

Such also was *Cyrus* King of Persia. Such was *Alexander* the great, til he began to waxe idle (as not hauing whereupon to exercise his prowesse) and to giue ouer his life to drunkennesse and incontinency. Suche was *Philippe* the Father of *Alexander*. Such was *Agesilaus*: *Themystocles*, *Simon*, *Aristides*, and other most famous Captaines amongst the Greekes. Such were the *Metelli*, the *Fabij*, the *Scipiones*, & such was *Pompeius*: and many other most renowmed Cheefteynes amongst the Romanes.

Such was *Mythridates* the most valiant and warlike
king

Militarie profession. 39

king of Pontus: and such was *Pyrrhus* king of Epyrus.

Such was *Iulius Cæsar*, the most worthie and best renowmed martialist of the world. Such were also *Octauius Augustus, Marcus Anthonius Pius, Alexander seuerus*: and many other renowmed Emperours, kinges, and Cheefteins amongst the olde heathen. And by these vertues they prospered in Armes, and became great in the world: & vnder the gouernment, nourishment, and protection of them, flowrished science, honest exercises, and ciuill policies.

Amongst the Israelites and Christians are also to be remembred in dutifull loue and honour, many Emperours, kinges and princes, endued with plentie of high and most noble vertues, and as they excelled in Armes, so were they riche in wisdome and goodnes, to the great benefite of the world, to the euerlasting praise of themselues, and eke to the glorious reliefe & aduancement of the knowledge and honour of God vpon earth: which without the zeale, industrie, wisdome and prowesse of noble princes had bene in hazarde to make vtter shipwracke many hundreth yeres past. And of these, are chiefly to be renoumed with sacred reuerence, & perpetual thansgiuing to our good God, *Moses*, the first ruler & captaine of the speciall people & Army of the Lord God of hosts. Then *Iosua. Othniel, Gedeon, Samson, Iephthe Samuel*, & *Deborah* the woman. Thē *Dauid*, the most acceptable & worthy captain & prophet, gods special & chosen king ouer his people Israel, by whose mightie value & martial prowesse, ÿ Lord stretched forth the kingdom of *Iacob*, to the promised bounds: & being a terror to the enemies of *Israel* abrode, & a chastiser of the rebels & hypocrites at home he, stablished peace & Iustice in *Israel*, and applied his wisdom, zeale, trauaile and treasure to aduaunce the honour, trueth, and true worshipping of God & his couenant in all the common wealth of *Israel*: which he pursued with such indeuor & integrity of hart,

Israelites that excelled in Armes.

E 4 that

that all things so prospered in his hand to the glorie of the Lorde, and to the health and wealth of Israel: that (in that respect) the Lorde saide: that He had found Dauid his seruant, a man after his owne heart.

Such also were *Zedekiah, Iosaphat,* and *Iosias,* renowmed in the Scriptures of God.

With these are to bee numbred (though not in that preeminencie) many Princes of the Christians, greatly endued with wisdome, ciuill vertues, and prowesse: which euer goe together, woorking the effecte of peace and prosperitie, in all places where they dwell in vse and power. Amongst such are chiefly to be named *Constantine* the great, *Charles* the great, and manye more Emperours of the olde time: and nowe lately, *Charles* the fifth: neyther is the last *Ferdinando* cast out of the Catalogue of good Princes: for he was very learned, desirous of peace, meeke, and modest, and liberall to honest desertes.

<small>Kings of high prowesse and vertues.</small>

Of the French kings, manye were of high prowesse vertues and value, & great nourishers of liberall Sciences. As were *Charles martel, Lewes* the pitious, *Philip Augustus,* the holy *Lewes, Philippe* the fayre, *Philippe de Valois. Iohn, Charles* the fift. *Charles* the sixt, a very sufficient Prince till he became Lunatike, *Charles* the seuenth, *Lewes* the eleuenth, *Charles* the eyghth, *Lewes* the twelfth, and *Frances* renowmed for his prowesse, modestie, prudence, and for his affection and aduancement of lerning, commonly called, The Father of Sciences. Then succeeded his Sonne King *Henrie,* a prince of high value in Cheualrie, gratious to his people, and bountifull to his friendes, and very readie to gratifie the deserts of men, and to aduance men of worthinesse, and in Armes most valiant.

And considering what rebellious and furious people the French are: it is to be wondered, that the prudence and industrie of their kinges was continually able to
represse

Militarie profession.

presse to refourm, and to reconcile so mutinous and rageous a natiō, as they haue alwais shewed themselues to be, molesting, vering, and spoyling the King, the gouernement, and common welth, by peopetuall vproses, continuing in Armes. Pillage, murthers, horrible massachres and disloyaltie (in some ages) three score yeres together. As in the dayes of King *Iohn*, *Charles the fifth*, *Charles the sixth*, & *Charles the seuenth*, which approueth great fidelitie, prowesse, and prudence, in the gentlemen, nobilitie, and bandes of warre: by whose value, so implacable and mad rebelles could be repressed and the state reformed.

Of the Kings of England bene also many renowmed amongst the good Princes: And hee of them that exceeded in military feates and prowesse, the same verely (as I haue often saide) excelled also, in wisedome, iustice, and ciuill vertues. As did *Arthur* amongst the Brutes. *Edmonde*, *Edgar*, *Athelston*, *Edwarde* and *Edwarde* amongste the Saxons. And since the conquest: *William* the conqueror himselfe, *Henry* the second, *Richard* the first, *Edward* the first, *Edwarde* the thyrde, *Henry* the fifte, and *Henry* the seuenth, and *Henry* the eighte.

Of Spayne King *Pelláyo*: and some others: but lastely and cheefly *Fernando* the fifth, the first entire Monarch of Spayne, that by his noble wisedome and passinge value in Armes, recouered the kingdome of Granado from the Mores: toke the kingdome of Naples, helde Sicilia in peace, and possessed the Indias.

Then *Charles*, that aduanced the honor and state of Spayne to the full summe: by vertue of military industrie and martial prudence, became renowmed amonge the most warrelike Princes of the worlde.

Now omittinge the famous Kinges and Princes of other countries and nations, for that I haue inferred

F. authorities

Renowmed Kings of England.

The defence of

authorities sufficient in force and number, to approoue and to magnifie the prayse of Armes: and to auoide more tediousnesse then here needeth: I will summe vp the Catalogue of renowmed Princes, with the sacred memory of them that are most worthie to be praised among the Christians of these dayes, for the incomparable value of their prowesse and warres, as due vnto the speciall martialists of the Lord God of hostes, by whose Armes, he did put in foot to fight with Sathan in plain battell, for the recouerie of his holy Sanctuary, that lay many a tedious yeere trodden vnder the féete of Antichrist: and earst durst not be attempted, till the Lorde had prouided his Army, and appointed his Checfteynes of courage, fayth, and Militarie prudence, fitte for the wars of *Iacob*. As were *Fredericke, Iohn*, and *Maurice*, the renowmed Princes in honour, chiualrie, and vertues, Dukes of Saxoni: *Philippe Lantgraue* of Hesse: *Albert Marques* of Brandenbourgh, *Christopher* Duke of Wyrtembergh, the warlike and faythfull states of Germany and Zurik. The Nobility of France, and aboue them al, *William*, Earle of Nassau, the vertuous, good, and happie Prince of Orange. By vertue of the fayth, industry, and prowesse, of these sacred martialists, is the gospell, and kingdome of Christ Iesus, brought againe to their passage, & fréely preached to the world, an inspeakable comfort & riches to al mankinde, and that specially to the elect children of God, to whom be prayse, Amen.

[margin: Renowmed princes of our age.]

These Militarie men being the most renowmed, the most sacred, beneficiall, and profitable personages of the world: to the worlde, and to all that dwell, and haue dwelled vpon earth, and that by warlike industrie: It must be granted, that al their assistants, and adherents: by whose labours, perils, blood, and valiancie, the great effects of Armes haue bene wrought: must bee comprehended in the same, and honour of their Princes, as a matter iustly to be imparted to euery one, according to

the

Militarie profession. 43

the value of his worthines: wherein the Romanes vsed orderly distributions of aduancemēt, & graces to ech on, as the prowesse & noblenesse of the Souldiers deserued.

The nature and due honour, of Militarie profession being such: what meaneth the vulgare multitude of the English Nation, so maliciously to contemne soldiership, and so brauely to despise the profession of Armes, as a vile, and damnable occupation: Surely, bicause they are of seruile and vnnoble heartes: foolish in discretion, idle bellies, carelesse of the common welth of their countrie, litle friendly to mankinde in generall, and lesse zealous toward the glory and preseruation of their Soueraigne Prince and gouernement. Howe be it they may seeme to voide this rebuke with a sleight, in denying to contemne Militarie profession: for they honor the, profession, and doe accordingly esteeme of all them that worthily pursued the same: But to despise the common sort of our Countriemen that go to warre, of purpose more to spoyle, then to serue: and as vnder colour of pursuite of Armes, they put themselues to the libertie and vse of swearing, dronkenes, shameles fornication, dicing, and theeuery, in slowe warres, & vnder loase gouernment in the tumultuous state of a forrein nation, where they thinke it a foolishe scrupulositie, to vse either tendernes of conscience, or yet any honest maners: So doe they returne into their Countrie, so much corrupted with all maner of euils, that they seeme rather to comefrom hel, then from the exercise of warlike armes, or frō the regiment of militarie discipline: & therefore so venemous a brode to their natiue countrey (standing in ciuill peace and gouernement) that they are rather to bee vomited out of the bulke of the common wealth, then to be nourished in the same. To contemne such (say they) yea, to abhor them as ẏ shame of martial armes, & to cut them of, as ẏ most infectiue nest of domestical society, is both honest & necessary by al ciuil, & diuine policy, & discretiō.

Dissolute soldiers ar worthely despised.

F 2　　And

And as for those that are worthely called martialistes, bearing the true forme and substance of military men, they (say our people) are highely to bee esteemed and maineteyned as the honorable and necessary membres of the state publique.

If the contemners of martiall Armes did keepe themselues within the compasse of these reasones and discretion, they coulde not bee iustely reproued: for the wicked in his wickednes is not to bee defended, bicause he professeth chiualry, or bicause he is a diuine. Let the euil therefore beare the blame and shame of his owne trespasse, and let the profession that is honorable in it self nature, goe vnuiolat, though al the professors of the same shoulde stande rightly reproued. If all the Preachers of the word of trueth and saluation were corrupt bellies: yet standeth the heauenly doctrine true and perfit in his own qualitie. Militarie occupation doth execute the high Iustice of God vpon earth, though all the followers of the same were most horrible & wicked (as the greater number of thē is) yet must the occupation by it selfe propertie stand honorable in the world, as the two edged sworde of the Lord God of hostes, to whom al Scepters & swordes doe perteine, and by his power and direction are vsed to effect.

The profession of Armes is honorable though some professours stand rightly vnreproued.

Now let vs examine the matter to trie whether these contemners doe directly despise the verie selfe profession of Armes, or noe. If they doe not, then doe they fauor it: and grantinge it to bee commendable and necessarie, they desire to practise the vse thereof in their domesticall pastymes and exercises: they couet the company of such as can instruct them in the same: they are prouided of habilements for the purpose, they loue honest Souldiers, & are frendely to them: they put themselues forth to the publike shew & practise before the presence of the royal maiesty and the nobilitie: they striue in emulation to excel in the redines & knowledg

of

Militarie profession. 45

of Military order, and in the vse of their weapons: they desire to serue against the intestine disturbers of the State publike, and couet to fight against the inuaders of their countrie: and are liberall in contributing to the charges of warres. But when the prince commandeth Musters through the realme in citie, towne, and country, and to appointe selecte people to be numbred and deuided into bands, for to be practised and exercised in the vse and order of Armes, that thereby the realme may bee the better furnished of Militarie men for the fielde, and thereby stand in the more assurance if neede of warre shall happen: for the hoste of an vnskilfull multitude in Armes, is before an Armie of experimented warriours, as a flocke of sheepe before a troupe of wolues: which consideration should moue honest heartes feruently to desire to be of profitable value for this occupation: wherein consisteth the preseruation of the soueraigne maiestie, and of the state publike: and consequently of euery particular state and person comprehended in the same.

If then I say, the rurall man, by bribes, by a liuerie Coate, by franke laboured friendship, by counterfaite sickensse, or by starting from his house vnder colour of farre busines, doth shifte himselfe from the ordinances of the prince, in so high and prouident direction: hee is not onely to bee counted a contemner of Armes, but is also (whether he be gentleman, or yeoman) to be rebuked with discredit, eyther as a slouthfull cowarde, or els to be punished with stripes, as a traiterous contemner of his soueraigne prince and country. If the citizen or townesman, doe inlike wise put forth his apprentice, his seruaunt, or poore hireling, to supply his place, and to withdraweth his owne person from the royall ordinances being himself of cõmendable sufficiencie in body had it an honest heart) he is to be noted, eyther a fearefull cowarde, and dare not deale with Armes, or els a

Contemners of Arme

F 3 slouthfull

slouthfull beast, or els in the abundance of his welth, in the height of his proud countenance, or in the opinion of his grauity: a dispiser of so contemtible a state, as to march with a Caliever, or a Pike on his backe in the rankes of poore souldiers (men stripped in light clothes, bearing their tooles in their hands, ready at every moment to be offered vp in the praise of martiall prowesse, for the seruice of their prince & countrye) & consequently, disdaineth the profession, and beareth a faint courage toward his soueraigne prince & country: & therefore not to be accepted amongst the men of sounde loyalty, & honorable value: no thogh his riches be neuer so much. He (whatsoeuer state or profession he be of) ÿ hath liuer bestow fiue poūdes on a superfluous banket, to fill ÿ gluttonish wombs of greasy swine ÿ are ouer fat, rather thē a shilling on a destitute soldier: he is no louer of Armes.

<small>The description of them that be no louers of Armes.</small>

He that will rather bestowe ten thousand pound on a purchase, then giue his xl.s. toward the furnishing of an honest minded poore gentleman to the warres: the same is no louer of Armes.

He that seeth a mā of good ablenes, distressed with nakednes, & hunger, begging his relief, & wandring in miseries, without home or harborogh: & rather then he wil comfort them with a Testone, would bestow fiue poūds on the lyning of a sōmer gowne, & fiue thousand poūdes to purchase leases ouer the heads of the poore, & to builde vp olde rotten tenements of the new, ÿ he may enhance the rents thereof: that fellow is no louer of armes, but a caterpiller in the orchards, and a noysull swine in the meddowes of the common welth of his countrie.

He that wil rather bestow a hundreth poūds on building of a banketting house in his garden, then a hundreth shillings in a subsidie to ayde the charges of his prince in the affaires of his country: the same surely, (if any such be in England) is no louer of Armes: neither hath he any fancie to militarie exercise.

He

Militarie profession.   47

He that had rather hang twenty able men for smal offences (forced through the extreame oppression of miserable want) then to relieue on distressed body, & to plant him in state to liue without euil shiftes: surely the same man is no louer of Armes. For he that loueth Armes, loueth men also: & he that acknowledgeth the honor and value of warlike profession, wil be tender ouer the liues of men: and will therefore open his purse to helpe the distressed: lest through want he fal to euill & perdition..

Looke so many of our nation as are tainted with these faults, & such like, are contēners of armes, & consequently no faithful friends or louers of their prince & country, & likewise improuident toward their own priuate state: for where ȳ common welth is in hazard, there ȳ coward & the couetous are in one asturāce: & where ȳ state publike maketh wrack, there doth perish ȳ louer of himself, & the foolish contemner of armes also. For the state & nation that is not able to stand in arms, & to vanquish the rage & power of both intestine & forrein violence, ȳ same is sure to be reuenged vnder the oppression & lust of the spoilers, at one time or other: & then go al things to hauock, the gold of the couetous, & the mony of the vsurer, the deintye wife, & the tender daughter, ȳ delicate sonne made a slaue, ȳ proud & rich father loden with giues, clothed with vermin, & fed with penury, & beatē w stripes, til he gree to redeeme himselfe with a greater ransome then he is euer able to satisfie. The gay houses with the winter parlours, and sommer parlours, with the inner Chambers, and the vtter, consumed with flames, and the whole Citie with fire: their streetes and fieldes lying couered with the deade carkeises of them that contemned prowesse, and had Armes in derision: the wiues and children wandering harbourlesse without honour, or succour, bestowe their carkeises amongest the ashes, and ruines of their desolate habitations, and in the Bushes, the infant likewise with his mother, starue

[margin:] The estate of that countrey is ruinous that is not able to stand in Armes.

with

with hunger and nakednesse. These dreadfull matters, made ye wise Lacedemonians, to bring vp al their youth in harde diet, thinnely clothed, poorely bedded: extreemely holden in the practise of difficult feates, in labour of the bodie, in the feates of actiuitie, and vnder the practise and rudimentes of militarie weapons and orders: that in all points they might be perfectly fashioned for the warres.

The Lacedemonians bringing vp.

The like considerations made the Romanes to pursue the exercise of warre (for many yeares at the foundation of their state) without wages or stipende: and whilest they did growe, there was neuer Citizen in *Rome* esteemed noble for his riches, but for his prudence & prowesse. Nay, the man of *Rome* that omitted armes, and became a merchant, for gathering of aboundance of riches, was rather reckoned amongst the seruaunts, then esteemed as a very Romane.

The French also do not esteeme a merchant worth thousandes, so much as they do a valiant souldier not worth a Testone in wealth. So in Germany, & likewise in Spaine, howbeit, the Lawier, and Merchant, the Rustique, and Clearke, that by honest bountie and frendly grace towarde Martialistes, doe shewe them selues to be louers of armes, and to honour warlike prowesse: are in their vocation greatly to be worshipped and praysed. But the merchauntes and Lawyers of most countries in the continent, thinke not so to satisfie the desire of their owne credite and estimation, or so to accomplishe their bounden loyaltie towarde the state publique: that by their fauour & liberalitie towards men of warre, it were seemely & lawful for them to withdraw themselues from the pollice and vse of armes: and therfore doe labour to be skilfull in the vse of warlike weapons, and in the pollicies eke, and orders of the warre, and stand) ech accoording to his ability) alway furnished for the feelde, as the merchants, & Citizens in high *Alther*

Militarie profession. 49

maine, are horsemen: the Artificers are footemen. Neyther doe the citizens of high Almaine, that are of segnioritie and worshippe, euer walke abrode in the streets, without their Swordes by their sides: For where the men of chiefe rule and creditte in a citie, doe leaue of the vsual wearing of domestical weapons, within their owne iurisdictions, there seemeth the state or citie to be vanquished and subdued to an Armed ruler, that for auoiding of mutinies and rebellions, forbiddeth the inhabitants to beare any Armorie.

Well, this discourse may seeme more tedious then auaileable: for it is harde to teache an olde horse to manach: so is it nothing hopefull, to see the secure rustikes, and dayntie citizens of England, faithfully to fauour the pursuite of Armes, much lesse to practise the vse and skill thereof: For say they, it belongeth not vnto them, neither doth the state of our Countrie (and as they hope it shall not) stand in any such neede, that men of credit, of worshippe, and of wealth, should be driuen to enter the occupations of Souldiours: for their purses shall serue the turne.

If they will aunswere men so, I will reason a litle farther with them, letting then to vnderstande more plainely, the improuidence and straightnesse of their heartes: for these reproueable shiftes cannot proceede but from a minde specially corrupted with three great faultes: the one is Auarice, the other is Selfe loue, the third is very disdain, & (as I haue said) a very great contempt of the profession it selfe: which haue no dwelling places, but in harts wanting wisdome, and all the parts of high and vertuous noblenesse.

They that mak shifts not to beare armour are corrupted with three vices.

If these men would lift vp their eyes from the greedy desire of fleshly lust, and set their heartes at libertie from the wretched bondage of seruile loue to this present worlde and to the vanities thereof, and discreetly consider the alterations and troubles of all the States,

G king-

kingdomes, and nations of the continent, throughout all the whole flower of the olde Romane Empire, and how things doe dayly more and more encline to dangerous and dreadfull chaunges, and then conclude that England also (though in the middest of the great Ocean) is a worldly state and kingdome, subiect (as the rest are) to the vncertenty of peace & prosperity, standing renged withall the world, vnder the sword of Gods high iustice: and therefore, doubt the fraile felicity of their Countrie, and accordingly haue care and regard to the same. Then would they vse the endeuors of wise hearts, then would they loue vertue, embrace godlines, honor Armes, and consequently prouide and furnishe themselues (eche one after his habilitie) of those habilements y are behoueful and necessary for couert & defence, in the day when the Lord shall visite the pride and security of men, powring out the tempest of is wrathfull indignation, eyther by forren: or intestine war, or els by both: which doth orderly fal at one time or other, vpon all and euery nation vpon earth, so y not one citie of the whole worlde can scape the araignement of the most high, when hee setteth him down to iudge. The armour that saueth all men, and nations from the dint and dart of the enemy, is a sure faith, an humble feare, sounde loue and trust in the Lorde God of hosts, through Christ Iesus our Lord, that great conquerour, king of kings, Lord of Lords. The wisdom eke and prowesse that doth make a man pollitike in warres, is heauenly contemplation, and a righteous hearte maketh the souldier inuincible in the battell: adding vnto these matters, the iron armour, the sword, the speare, the shield, and the horse, the corslet, and the pike, the murrian, and the caliuer, the bowe and the bill: with the requisite skill, courage, industrie and agilitie that doe appertcine vnto the vse of the same. The citie or kingdome that is stored of men, furnished with these habilements, may well set foorth an armie, compleate in armes, hopefull

Militarie profession. 51

full of victorie, and assured of triumph.

Of such a suite of Militarie men, consisted the hostes of *Moses*, and *Iehosuah*, and *Gedeons* three hundreth, by whose prowesse he vanquished the mightie and dreadfull Armie of the enemies of *Israel*. When *Iacob* was appointed with any captaines, and bands of this Militarie perfection: then went the Lorde God of hostes with their Armies into the fielde: then were they sure to vanquish their enemies, and to returne to their houses with a ioyfull victorie: For one true Israelite was able to driue a thousande Philistims to the flight. Such a Souldier was *Ionathas*, and such was *Caleb*, and his sonnes: such was *Dauid*, and his worthie men, and such was also *Iudas Macchabeus* and his brethren.

The Midianites vanquished by Gedeon.

These were the good children of God: most valiant, and most famous in warlike prowesse: For by vertue and armes, they became inuincible in the field, and most profitable in the citie. The christiā therfore, that desireth to be worthily reckned amongst the honorable, praised of the honest, & esteemed with the wise & faithful sort: ỹ same must in martiall armes, & eke in heauenly vertues, be a compleate Israelite. This being true, (as it is a heauenly trueth, and cannot be repugned, without the contempt of the high maiesty of the lord God of hostes) let euery citizen & rurall man, gentle or vngentle, noble or vnnoble, riche or poore, that meaneth to proue himself a good christian, a faithful Englishman, zealous toward the state publike of his coūtry, of cōmendable integrity toward his prince and feruent in the loue and maintenance of Gods kingdome and glory vpon earth: let euery such one I say, imbrace godlinesse: honour, nourish, and exercise Armes, and learne with diligence, the skill and prudence that doe necessarily accompany the same.

Though the purses of the riche, doe sufficiently serue ỹ turne in furnishing forth others, to serue in their steede in these warres, ỹ seeme rather voluntary or politike, thē

G 2 dangerous

daungerous to the state publike of their Countrie: yet should they eche in his order, and sense, couet to knowe the pollicies and discipline of warre: and so desire, and voluntarily put foorth themselues, to aduaunce Militarie knowledge and actiuitie, that they would rather beseeche the Souereigne Maiestie, to giue them liberty to practise the feelde vpon their free courage and charges, then to tarie the commaundement and direction of the Prince for the same, and then doe it so vnwillingly, as I will not speake, and so contemptuously, that the seruant and hireling is preferred to serue the ordinances of the Prince, whereby that good pollicie and purpose of the soueraigne Maiestie is greatly deceiued, and the pretended prouidence should (by this fraud) be poorely satisfied in the day of seruice, as neede might possibly happen. For if ciuill discord should rise, and the realme fall to Armes (as it is a rife matter) who were fittest to defende the Throne of the royall Maiestie, the Iudgement seate and the Citie, the Cradle, and Pulpit? Surely they that are likeliest, of fayth, credite, and habilitie: therefore, are euen they to be committed to the practise and trust of Armes: For in the day of tumult, the armed seruant wil be a comander of his vnarmed master, and the armed Sonne will be a terror to the vnarmed Father. Then wil the drudge and seruile man, the hireling, and fugitiue person, starte from his Musters, and ioyne himself with the mutiners: for vnto such the hope of common spoyle, and the desire of ruinous theft and libertie, is more delicate then the defence of ciuil gouernment, or the preseruation of the weale publike: which should moue them to preferre themselues, and not their seruants, to the practise and profession of Armes.

what danger may ensue by preferring hirelings to the seruice of warre.

Let London therfore, the royall Chamber, and head of the state, appeare to loue Armes, and endeuor themselues to aduance the knowledge & practise of the same: and as they are more prudent, more honorable, more
mightie,

mightie, & more able then any state, or particular countrey els within the Realme, and most conueniently associated and vnited together, to enter, and to erect the familiar & domesticall practise of Military knowledge & actiuity: so shuld they be an example & an encouragemēt to al the rest of ye cōminalty, to immitate thē with honest emulatiō, through the fauor & authority of ye soueraigne maiesty, ye same being admitted to ye people of honest state & credit, & likeliest in ciuil towardenes. So shoulde London be more honorable then earst it hath ben, and the nation strong and prudent against the day that those vertues might happe to stande them in better steede then much riches, and more auailable to the common welth, then al the lawe and merchandise in the lande.

For methinketh that it is poore thing and a verie ignominious to see so large and rich a city, so populous of select and passing manry, to bee so ignorante and so naked of warrelike adress and endeuours. The Frenche citizins are furnished and practised for the feelde, so are the youthes, their sonnes and seruantes. The citizens of Italy doe striue to excelle the nobilitie in the knowledge and feates of Armes. The citizines of Germany professe Armes, and are accordingly exercised and furnished for the same. *Citizens should be furnished and practised for the feelde.*

In the litle citie Geneua, are 5000. citiziens of ordinary bandes sworne in Armes: redy at a call in euerye moment. In Strasbourgh are likewise 8000. citizens redye to Armes at a cal: the like in Ausburge, in Norynbergh, and after the same maner in all other cities of Germany, and the East Countries, ech in adress, and appointment of Militarie forces, according to their largenesse, & habilitie. And is London so sure that it needeth not the very simple knowledge of Armes? and is it so carelesse that it despiseth the exercise of the feelde, as a matter nothing apperteining vnto them? Such slouth, and securitie hath brought many a famous citie of the worlde to ruine, desolation, and seruitude. London *Defence of cities.*

might often times (in her life dayes) haue bene brought to the same predicament, had not their kings bene at hand, to stoppe and to vanquishe the insolencie of ragious rebbels, by the force of Armes. The sword of one noble citizen wonne more fame and honour to the citie of London, in killing the arrogant rebbell *Iacke strawe*, then euer it had afore: and for that worthie fact, the Maiors of London, are adorned with knighthood, which is an honour properly perteining to chiualry: not to marchandise, nor to any other occupation, nor yet to the aboundance of riches.

<small>VVherefore the Maiors of London are adorned with knighthood.</small>

If they then, and their ancesters, citizens of London, are beholding to Military prowesse, for the chiefe honour & ancient (yea, and newe) preseruation of their citie: why do they not honour the profession, & desire libertie of their prince, to practise armes, and to nourishe Militarie practise amongst themselues? Their approued loyaltie shall not faile to obteine that grace of their blessed Queene. Then should London be martial against the day of war, and able vpon the sodaine to put it selfe in armes (the soueraigne prince and nobilitie being farre of, and otherwise entangled) for the repression of domestical mutinies if any should happen nere them, or towarde them: As all rebels haue their chief purpose to make hauok of Lōdon.

It were a small matter for the citie of London to haue fiue thousand citizens of special manry, trained in arms, booked, and deuided into bands, and ready at a moment, if néed were: in which number, should no seruant nor fugitiue person bee admitted, but the very housholders, and their sonnes: neither were it much for them to haue fiue hundreth furnished & exercised horses for the field. *Anthony Fugger*, the great money master of all Christendome, kept alwayes fiftie horses of seruice in his owne stables in Augusta, and so many warlike chosen Reisters of his owne family. This number of trained people being euer redy to be leuied out of one citie at the sodeine commandement

<small>Anthony Fugger.</small>

Militarie profession.

ment of their prince vpon sodeine occasion, might serue to a greater purpose, then twenty thousande long in gathering, and them of rude and ignorant rurall people.

And to speak in general, pity it is to see so worthy a nation as ours is (so valiant & actiue in arms, when they be entred in y exercise therof) to be so poorely inclined to follow wars, & to cōtinue the pursuit of chiualry: y punishment therfore of our idle people cannot be to extreeme: so that there were a sufficient order set down for y employment of them. But to say truely, let the soueraigne maiesty & the court of parliament, prouide & establish neuer so easie, & neuer so profitable & seemly means for the succour of the poore, & for imployment of the able people, this nation wil not obserue it: such slouth & corruption is in the Iustices of the country, & in the magistrates of townes & cities, & eke such peruers obstinacie in the merciles harts of rich folke, both of towne and country, that euery mans endeuor wholly tendeth to his owne priuate profit, that of al hands they neglect, yea, & contemne y publike welth & honour of their country: much lesse do they regard the preseruation of the poore: so dul & senseles is the common sort of this nation: neither will it bee remedied for any thing that can be deuised or commanded, til God himself do remedy it with a scourge of his owne making. Fiue persons standing at the barre condemned to dye vpon the statute of Rogues, & vpon no other matter, proclamation was made in the ful appearance of the country, that if any would come forth and take any one of the condemned, and reteine him in seruice, & answere for his behauiour, he should deliuer a man from death, in all the throngs of the people there was not one moued with compassion so to doe, then were all these miserable wretches executed: surely a hard condition amongst the people that professe Christ: whose commandement it is, that as we are his, so must we loue one another as he loued vs.

Christ committed his body to the shamefull Crosse, & his

his soule to the tormentes of hell, for the redemption of trayterous Rebbels against the high Maiestie of God, and to reconcile the wicked to grace: and willeth vs to be mercifull, as our Heauenly Father is mercifull. But how farre we are from these qualities, the Lord he knoweth it, and so doe the poore. God surely will iudge it with a heauie sentence.

But surely, this is a true conclusion, that the man, the people, or nation that fauour not the renowme and maintenance of Military prowesse, nor imbrace the high value of Armes, the same are enemies to all vertues, neyther haue they respect to godlinesse: but all to their owne bellies, as the swine. If the nourishment and practise of Armes should depende on the voluntarie charges and endeuours of the common multitude, Martiall profession should lye in the streete, vntill it were trodden to dunge.

In deede it is not a matter that doth properly apperteine to base & seruile mindes, but doth belong to the noble and ambitious courages. Let them therfore that are truely noble, loue Armes, and let them that chalenge, or loue the name of honour, vertue, honestie, or worthines, put their hands to the vse and aduancement of warlike knowledge and actiuitie: yea, the more noble, the more prudent, and honorable that men will bee esteemed, so much the more friendly to Armes ought they to be, and the like delightfull in the practise and vse of the same.

And as they esteeme of it, so to esteeme of them that do applye the occupation thereof in the feelde, where they suffein no wanton labour, but are in continual trauail of the body, and eke of the minde, dayly presented to the daungers of death: whose hourely appearaunce to the Martialist in Armes, shoulde make him to consider the frailtie of his state, and the fewnesse of his dayes, and therefore to apply his heart to wisdome, and vertue, and to be alwayes, as a man prepared, and ready to be sacri-
ficed:

Militarie profession. 57

ficed: yet when the secure bellie doth rest vpon an assured hope of long life: and hating the remembrance of death, hideth himselfe from the sight of wisdome, and geueth ouer his [heart to lust and couetousnesse, the mother and nourse of all euils.

If any tongues more malicious, then discreet, will disable our martialists, and defame our souldiours, and then make a false conclusion, against the profession it selfe: let those malignant spirites confesse the renowmed value of our nation in the olde time, and grant (in spight of their beards) that we are the sonnes of those our Fathers, whose strength and courage in martiall actiuitie, neither Scots, French, nor Spanyards, were able to resist: nor yet safely to stand within the compasse and industrie of the Captaines: and that this present generation of the English people, being trained and exercised vnder the like conduct, nourishment, & gouernment as our kindred were vnder the moste famous kings, *Richard* the first, *Edward* ÿ first, *Edward* the third, *Edward* the blacke Prince, *Henry* the fifth, the Duke of Bedford, &c. wold shew it self to be the rightfully begotten children of the olde English Fathers, most valiant and famous in Militarie feates and knowledge: yea, looke how much more subtile and perilous the warres at these dayes are, then they were in the olde time: by so much the more shoulde we exceede our ancesters in the affaires of the same, if wee were accordingly imployed and mainteined.

Englishmen by training vp, the most valiant and famous in martiall feates and knowledg

Let therefore, the gratious Nobilitie of England (Fathers to their Prince, people, and common wealth) remember, that as martiall profession must of necessitie bee vsed and nourished, that euen the followers of the same must be likewise esteemed and mainteined: and eke to set downe an arrest, for the domesticall practise of the same. *Vsus enim promptos facit.* And that being continued through the Realme by such order and direction

tion, as may conueniently and sufficiently be proportioned and stablished: there should be within a few yeres, many thousandes of able Souldiers in England, that neuer saw enemie in the field: and that with smal charges to the Soueraigne Maiestie.

And as all Souldiers of worthinesse and knowledge are to bee highly esteemed and mainteined, so are the gentlemen, and worthie people of our nation that haue pursued the defensory warres in the lowe Countrie, specially to be praised: for they haue approued that the olde English valiancy is not so extinguished in the English nation through long securitie, and corrupt idlenesse, but it is soone stirred vp to a double force, when it hath a while acquainted it selfe with the exercise of the fielde.

Record of their seruice in Brabant against the Spaniards, vpon Lammas day last: where the Commanders shewed commendable value of prudence and courage, and in likewise the common seruitours, honest hardinesse, and worthy actiuity: and are therefore to be cherished for their owne deserts, and eke to bee esteemed for the encouragement of others.

And for that I haue here made mention of the seruice of our nation in Brabant, that it may bræde further encouragement vnto others that are likewise wel minded vnto Martial occupatiō: I haue thought good briefly to set downe the maner of their seruice done at the same time, that the worthy acts of those valiant & worthy captaines and souldiers, may remain a prowfe of the value of the English nation, and shew that they are not so far degenerate from the high courage and manlines of their auncestors & forefathers, but that (if they were exercised and accustomed to the field & practise thereof) they woulde soone attaine and deserue their pristinate valiantnes, and so become a terror to their enemies, as their forefathers in times past haue bene.

It

Militarie profession. 59

It is to be noted, that the campe of the States of the lowe Countrie, lay entrenched in a great heath or sandie ground, on the right hand of whose campe towards Loueine there was a ryuer ranne all along, and without the trenches on the same side, was the Englishe and Scottishe mens warde, wherein was a hill that the Spanyardes layd hard at to haue gotten, which if they coulde haue wonne, from the same they might haue discryed all their maner of dealing in the States Campe. On the other side of the campe toward Askot, was another hill, vpon the which, the horsemen of the States kept scoutwatch, and betweene these two hils was a great valley of champion grounde, with some smal sandie hils at the entring into the plaine.

On the farther side of the plain, were certain houses, which the Englishmen set on fire, thereby to anoy the enemy. The horsemen of the States which lay in scoute vpon the hill, on the left hand, perceiuing the Armie of *Don Iohn* to approche out of the streight into the plaine, sent worde vnto the Captaines of the Englishmen and Scots, willing them to stande manfully to it that day against the enemie, and to doe their best, and they shoulde be assured that they woulde not forsake them, but liue and dye with them.

Whereupon the Chiefe commaunders of the Englishe and Scottishe regiments went to counsell, to take aduice for the ordering of their companies, and howe they might endomage the enemie, fully purposing to trie the value and courage of their enemies, for that such a brute had bene spreade ouer the worlde (but especially in all the lowe Countries) of their inuincible prowesse and knowledge in Martiall discipline, as though there were not any nation that durst encounter them in the fielde. After good aduice taken, euerie Captaine & officer was appointed to his charge for ye day, as some to stand in battel, some to lie in ambush, others to

H 2   relieue

relieue their fellowes w fresh shot, and some to furnish them that wanted shot and pouder: and the chiefe Coranels taking to them certaine valiant gentlemen, and a conuenient number of approued souldiers, determined to giue the onset vpon the enemy.

Betwixt nine and ten of the clocke in the morning, the horsemen of *Don Iohn* issued out of the streight, into the plaine & champion ground, whereupon the States horsemen (for what purpose, it was to vs vnknowne) retired within their trenches, and there abode vntill they saw which way the game went, and who had the better. The footmen also of the Spanyards, being entred into the plaine, the chiefe Coranels of the English and Scottishe regiments, taking to them those loose shotte which were before appointed, encoũtred the Spanyard's vpõ the plain, and delt so hotly and frankly with them at Pel Mel, that within three quarters of an houre they made them forsake the plaine, and retire ouer, into the fields, there nere adioyning: at the entrie whereof was many a man slaine, to the great discouragement of the whole Armie of *Don Iohn*, and the Spanyardes. Thus through the goodnesse of God (in whose quarrell they fought) for the aduancement of his name and true religion, and by the prowesse of those valiant English men that there serued vnder the States (whose noble harts sheweth forth a liuely patterne of the prowesse of their progenitors) with the aide onely of a few Scottish men that serued there also: so terrified the harts of the Spanyards, that amongst all the encounters that I haue sene in al the time that I haue serued, for these xxij. yeares, I neuer sawe enemies so danted with any losse or repulse as the Spanyards were that day, in flying the fury of the people, they being of so great strength, and our folke but a fewe loose shot. Then issued forth the *Graue van Bussu*, generall of the States armie, and stood vpon a litle hill, facing the horsemen of of *Don Iohn*, and vewing

The English and Scottishmen encounter the Spanyards at Pel Mel.

Militarie profession.

ing the maner of the skirmish. After that the Spanyards were thus driuen to forsake the plaine, and to retire into the closes neere adioyning, seeing the inuincible courage of our men, durst not any more come forth into the plaine, but now and then salyed out, and straight wayes retired in againe. About foure or fiue a clocke in the after nœne, the English and Scottish souldiers were so stirred vp, that they determined no longer to stande dallying with the Spanyardes, but purposed to forsake the plaine champion, and to follow the Spanyardes into the fieldes, and there to haue them by the eares. Don Iohn seeing his footmen were put to the worse, and fearing a further mischief, was driuen of necessitie to make a profer with his horsemen, but did not breake, which caused our men to stay their going ouer into the fields, so that in this meane while, the Spanish fœtmen (before the English & Scottish men were a ware) were a quarter of a mile off, retiring in running maner ouer hedge and ditch with their ensigns, and so ended the skirmish. The Coranels and captaines both of the Englishmen and Scots did lead the seruice themselues that day, with such great boldnesse, that it greatly imbased the glory and force of the Spanyards, and had vtterly ouerthrowen them, if the horsemen had done their endeuor halfe so well as did the footmen.

The Spanyards put to flight.

Thus gentle reader I haue briefly described the seruice of our countrimen vppon Lammas day last past, whose valiant seruice, for the exalting of the worde of God, & honor of their countrie, deserueth the fauourable liberalitie of all honest and louing harts, ẏ where occasion serueth and need requireth, they would reach forth their hands, and out of their plentie, relieue the necessitie of such pœre soldiers as haue aduentured their liues for the aduauncement of true religion: so shall others thereby be encouraged to imploy themselues in the like seruice, and be ready, and prest at all times to offer vp

H 3   themselues

themselues and their seruice in the defence of the quiet state and prosperitie of their prince and countrey: for these dayes are dangerous, and more dangerous will yet be.

  Honos enim alit artes.

  Let England therefore while it hath blessed rest and leasure, wise regiment, and God present in the Sanctuarie, waken it selfe out of senselesse securitie, and diligently looke to her Tacles: for a storme will come, and a tempest will fall: for at this present houre, the hand of the Lord God of hostes is in the seconde time for gathering together of the remnant of Israel: the yeere of his redeemed is come, and euery kingdome that wil not serue the Lord, shal vtterly perish from the earth: stand fast therefore, O ye people of England, for the sworde of the Almightie is drawne, and will not be put vp till hee hath confounded, and vtterly consumed all the enemies of Iacob from the face of the earth for euermore. Euerie vaine and misbelieuing soule is aduersary to Iacob, and it shalbe cut of. Serue the Lorde therefore in trueth of heart, and remember the wonderful benefites and blessings of God so abundantly bestowed vpon you, & vpon your fathers, and be thankful: for you and they haue enioyed your countrey many yeres in vniuersal peace, and in dayly increase of priuate and publike prosperity. The Lorde hath nowe twise deliuered you his Gospell without blood, and in this second restitution, he hath holden you twentie yeeres in the free occupation thereof, without murther or molestation: the Lord hath not so dealt with your neighbours, looke vpon the miserable state of France, and lowe Dutchland, and in the viewe therof consider the goodnes and prouidence of your heauenly Father towardes you: for their troubles haue nourished your rest, and their miseries haue continued your blessings. Sée into the procéedings of the Almighty,

            and

Militarie profession.   63

and be wise hearted, lest through lewde ingratitude you moue the Lord God of hostes to wrath, & through your rebellious insolencie, you prouoke the most high to forsake his Sanctuary in England: as they of Iudah and Ierusalem through their wickednes draue him to abandon his holy mounte Sion in the dayes of *Zedekiah*. But if the Lord depart from you, woe shalbe vnto you, as it was to them of Iudah and Ierusalem.

Looke wisely to your selues, and as ye loue the aduancement of Gods kingdome in England, so will you pray and labour for the prefermet of the same amongst the French & Dutch: as that the Lord may set his sanctuarie at rest amongst them as he hath done it amongst vs, and that they may haue the grace so to receiue, and so to reteine the Lord their God, as he may haue delight to continue with them.

As time draweth to his ende, and the corrupt world to her death, so shall all maner of euils abound amongst men: and these last dayes shalbe troublesome, daungerous and cruell, for the last drams of Sathan that must fill vp the measure of wickednesse to the brimme, shalbe most infectiue and pestiferous: be wise therefore, and acquainte your selues with armes, both corporal and spiritual, that you may at al times and in all causes be compleat Israelites ready for the fielde.
God grant it

The Lorde God of hostes blesse and preserue our good Queene ELIZABETH, the Nobilitie, people, and comminaltie of England. Lord, Amen.

FINIS.